LIVING IN COVENANT

Enjoying the Love, Freedom, Joy and Peace that is Every Christian's Inheritance

Basic teachings from the Bible that show us the fullness of life that every believer in Jesus Christ can come to know and experience.

Acknowledgment

Whilst not endorsing all his views, the author is grateful for the thoughts suggested in the talks on this subject by Bas Rijksen found on You Tube.

Most quotations from the Bible, are from
the New King James Version. (NKJV)

LIVING IN THE NEW COVENANT

Frederick Serjeant

This book is dedicated to all my former seminary students with thanks for the motivation they gave me to continue to study the Scriptures more deeply myself.

"O magnify the Lord with me, and let us exalt his name together"

Contents

Chapter 1

Introduction

If, dear reader, you do not as yet, think of yourself as being a professing Christian, I hope you will still read on. But this little book has been written particularly for those who do see themselves as Christians, whether very new believers or those who have been Christians for many years. By "Christians" – I mean those who have come to believe in the Jesus Christ as their personal Saviour, Redeemer and Lord. In other words, it is for those who know themselves to have been 'born again'.[1]

Now some readers may immediately write themselves off because this "evangelical stuff" is not their way of thinking. Others may begin to be

---

[1] John Chapter 3:1-21

put off because they don't know what it means, and have no idea of how someone is 'born again[2].

If, you happen to fall into either camp, I hope that before you dismiss what follows, you will go to Appendix A at the back and read that first.

The next thing to notice, is the footnotes back on page 9 and below. They refer to Bible references. The whole of this book is concerned with what **the Bible teaches** about the Christian life lived in the fullness of the grace and blessings of the New Covenant.

Again, there will be Christians who sincerely believe that they have been "born again' who will be wondering why we are emphasising the "New Covenant". The short answer to that is that there are many Christians today who seem still to have one foot in the Old Covenant! The teaching they have received has led them to think that this is normal. The result is that like those the apostle Paul wrote to in his letter to the Galatians, they

---

[2] See the Gospel of John Chapter 3 verse 1-21

are in danger of being *"entangled with a yoke of bondage"* (Galatians 5:1). They continue individually to be the "wretched man (or woman)" described by Paul in his letter to the Romans. (Romans 7:13-25 see especially verse 24).

To benefit from this little book you are going to need a Bible! If you don't have one, then you can download one from the Internet. [3] But it will be much better if you get yourself a printed copy. I suggest a New King James Version (NKJV). This is the version I shall usually be quoting from. But some may find the New International Version (NIV) more helpful, being a freer modern language version.

I suggest too, if you can afford it, that you buy one with a good flexible cover. A flexible cover makes it easier to quickly find a place or reference.

---

[3] I suggest www.bible.com

If you are not familiar with the Bible, then look at the Table of Contents near the front of your Bible, where it gives a list of the 66 Books that make up the Bible and shows on which page each book begins. Bible references give the name of the Book, then the Chapter, then the verse(s) e.g. John 3:16 means John's Gospel, Chapter 3 and verse 16. Look it up now and you will find the best known verse in the Bible.

Chapter 2

The Covenants

Those who have been Christians for some time may wish to skip the next section, which is intended for those who are new to the Bible.

As we have indicated, the Bible consists of a collection of sixty-six books. These are divided into two main sections. The first section is entitled "Old Testament" and the second "New Testament", with 39 books in the Old and 27 in the New.

I shall be using the words 'Old Testament' to mean the first 39 books (which **contain** the <u>Old Covenant</u> made through Moses – and much more besides). I shall be using the words 'New Testament' to mean the next 27 books of Scripture (which **contain** the <u>New Covenant</u> made in the blood of Jesus - and much more besides). When using the word 'covenant' I am referring to an actual covenant.

The Five Main Covenants

The word covenant means a solemn and binding agreement between two or more parties. God has made a series of key covenants that are found in the Scriptures.

1. The first was with Noah and all mankind after the Flood. (Genesis 9:9).

2. The second was with Abraham and his descendants (Genesis 15:1,18).

3. The third (later called the OLD covenant) was with Moses and Israel (Exodus 19:5) .

4. The fourth was with David and his descendants (2 Samuel 7.

5. The fifth by Jesus (which He called the NEW covenant) through His death on the cross. (Matthew 26:28) .

There are a number of other minor covenants in the Bible, but these five form the underlying structure, revealing the outworking of God's plan of salvation of a chosen number from the fallen sinful human race. The first four Covenants point to the fifth as the final one. (The whole Bible is really about Jesus Christ – see Luke 24:27.)

Two Particular Covenants

Of these five Covenants, two are shown to be particularly important. The first of these being the OLD covenant made with Israel as a nation, through Moses (see Exodus 19 and 20). Unlike the covenants that came both before and after it, it was a **bi-lateral** – a two-sided covenant. It was also a **conditional** covenant. God said to Israel,

IF you keep the laws I have given you, **THEN** I will bless you. **IF** you do not keep the laws I have given you **THEN** I will curse you.

As the apostle Paul points out in his letter to the Romans and especially in his letter to the Galatians, it was a WORKS covenant. In other words it was **conditional** in that it depended on the works, or the keeping, of the Law. The 'Law' referred to here, was the Law of Moses. Jews refer to it in the Hebrew, as the Torah. It consists of the whole of the first five books in our Bible. At the heart of this Law are the Ten Commandments that were written on tablets of stone. (see Exodus 20).

This covenant made with Israel was meant to be a temporary covenant "until Christ should come" (Galatians 3:20). When Christ, the Son of God came, he fulfilled all the requirements of the Law, living a perfect life as man. He then suffered and died on the cross establishing in his shed blood, a New Covenant with all who would believe on him, whether Jew or Gentile.

This NEW covenant was **uni-lateral** – a one-sided covenant. It was **unconditional.** God made promises without any conditions attached. It is seen therefore to be a covenant of GRACE. By 'grace' we understand that it is entirely unmerited on the believer's part. 'Works' are excluded. (See Ephesians 2:8,9)

No Mixing of the Two Covenants

It is important for us to recognise that the Old covenant and the New covenant cannot be mixed. The first was a covenant of 'works' made with Israel as a nation, the second is a covenant of 'grace' made with those from all the nations upon the earth who (by God's grace) believe **savingly** [4] on the Lord Jesus Christ as their Saviour, Redeemer and Lord. I emphasis the word 'savingly' because there are many who may believe that Jesus lived, died and rose again from the dead, but come short of **saving** faith. James tells us that the demons believe there is one

[4] By 'savingly' we mean that is actually the kind of faith that is effective, resulting in salvation.

God; and no doubt they believe in the historical events concerning the life of Jesus.

"Even the demons believe—and tremble!" James 2:19

To believe IN Christ, is something far more. It is to trust solely in the Christ crucified for **me**. That he lived a perfect life and then died on the cross in MY place, paying the penalty for MY sins. (This is further explained in Appendix A).

In the Introduction, we made the point that there were many true believers today who seem to be living with one foot in the Old Covenant. They believe themselves to be saved by grace alone, but having been 'saved' they must now do their best to please God by keeping the Law. To put it in another way, they believe themselves to be 'justified by faith' but 'sanctified' by law-keeping'.

Read what Paul wrote in his letter to the Galatians:

"O foolish Galatians! Who has bewitched you that you should not obey the truth, before whose eyes Jesus Christ was clearly portrayed among you as crucified? This only I want to learn from you: Did you receive the Spirit by the works of the law, or by the hearing of faith? Are you so foolish? Having begun in the Spirit, are you now being made perfect by the flesh? Have you suffered so many things in vain—if indeed it was in vain?" Galatians 3:1-4

If you have become enmeshed in this mixture of law and grace, then you can find your way out of the troubled waters that have hindered your progress in grace, into the clear calm water of the blessings of the Gospel of grace.

The Renewing of the Mind

How is this going to be brought about? The answer to this question is the whole aim of this little book!

In brief, it is by the **renewing** of our minds (Romans 12:2) through the Word of grace. In the following sections, I trust to give some guidance to help believers to know this transformation. For it brings us into the fullness of the blessings of the New Covenant.

"And do not be conformed to this world, but be transformed by the renewing of your mind, that you may prove what is that good and acceptable and perfect will of God." Romans 12:2

Come then, into the liberty in which Christ sets us free!

Paul in his letter to the Galatians compares life under the Old Covenant and life under the New Covenant to the son of a slave (or bond) woman - Hagar and the son of a free woman, Sarah:

Tell me, you who desire to be under the law, do you not hear the law? For it is written that Abraham had two sons: the one by a bondwoman, the other by a freewoman. But he who was of the bondwoman was born according to the flesh, and he of the freewoman through promise, which things are symbolic. For these are the two

20

covenants: the one from Mount Sinai which gives birth to bondage, which is Hagar— for this Hagar is Mount Sinai in Arabia, and corresponds to Jerusalem which now is, and is in bondage with her children— but the Jerusalem above is free, which is the mother of us all. For it is written:

"Rejoice, O barren, You who do not bear!

Break forth and shout, You who are not in labor!

For the desolate has many more children

Than she who has a husband."

Now we, brethren, as Isaac was, are children of promise. But, as he who was born according to the flesh then persecuted him who was born according to the Spirit, even so it is now. Nevertheless what does the Scripture say? "Cast out the bondwoman and her son, for the son of the bondwoman shall not be heir with the son of the freewoman." So then, brethren, we are not children of the bondwoman but of the free.

Galatians 4:21-31

Note also:

"Stand fast therefore in the liberty by which Christ has made us free, and do not be entangled again with a yoke of bondage. Indeed I, Paul, say to you that if you become circumcised, Christ will profit you nothing." Galatians 5:1,2

"So if the Son sets you free, you will be free indeed." John 8:36

"For the law of the Spirit of life in Christ Jesus has made me free from the law of sin and death." Romans 8:2

And having been set free from sin, you became slaves of righteousness. Romans 6;18

But now having been set free from sin, and having become slaves of God, you have your fruit to holiness, and the end, everlasting life. Romans 6:22

"For if anyone is a hearer of the word and not a doer, he is like a man observing his natural face in a mirror; for he observes himself, goes away, and immediately forgets what kind of man he was. But he who looks into the perfect law of liberty and continues in it, and is not a forgetful hearer but a doer of the work, this one will be blessed in what he does." James 1:23-25

Chapter 3

You Can Be Set Free

Those who know they have been born-again, may certainly know that they are not under the law but under grace:

"For sin shall no longer be your master, because you are not under the law, but under grace." Romans 6:14

Yet they also realise that they still retain some of the effects of their old life under the law. The memories and more importantly, the habits of thinking, have left their imprint on their minds.

Like instructions in computer programs, these must be over-written. Any attempt simply to erase them is doomed to failure. This explains one of the reasons why some find themselves trapped in habitual sin. The remedy is to be found in the Word of God. We all need to renew these former 'old man' thought patterns with God's 'new man' thoughts.

"But you have not so learned Christ, if indeed you have heard Him and have been taught by Him, as the truth is in Jesus: that you put off, concerning your former conduct, the old man which grows corrupt according to the deceitful lusts, and be renewed in the spirit of your mind, and that you put on the new man which was created according to God, in true righteousness and holiness." Ephesians 4:20-24

We need to change from a "law mind-set" to a "grace mind-set". A law mind-set deceives us into a "performance" life-style, forever striving to do things for God - instead of relying on the gifting of the indwelling Spirit to produce the fruit of the Spirit through us. (Galatians 5:22-25)

Two-Fold or Three-Fold Nature?

From the times of the ancient Greeks up to the present day, numerous philosophers and theologians have made the point that "Next to knowing God, the key to wisdom is knowing oneself.".

Do we know our own nature? How God has created it? To know how sin has affected it? How God has a plan to redeem it?

Christians have differed over their understanding of human nature in its unregenerate and in its regenerated state. Throughout the Dark Ages of the Church (from about AD 500 to AD 1500) the teaching was that man consisted of a **two-fold** nature - body and soul. This persisted in the teaching of some of the Reformers in the time of the Reformation (1450 – 1550). Notably, this teaching was embedded in much of the devotional writings of the Puritans.. Puritan teaching (1550-1650) has continued to have considerable influence on much Evangelical teaching right up to the present day..

However, other theologians and teachers have seen from Scriptures the full **three-fold** nature of man. I suggest that this is the better and more helpful way of perceiving ourselves.

In the Old Testament (Hebrew) Scriptures we have three words for the full three-part nature of man. Also in the New Testament (Greek) Scriptures we also have three words describing the full three-fold nature of man. These words are (or should be) translated as spirit, soul and body. We find them for example in 1 Thessalonians 5:23:

"Now may the God of peace Himself sanctify you completely; and may your whole spirit, soul, and body be preserved blameless at the coming of our Lord Jesus Christ".

To understand our own spiritual state it is important that we we see the difference between the (human) spirit and the soul.

Hebrews 4:12 shows us that it is by the Word of God that we discern the difference:

28

"For the word of God is living and powerful, and sharper than any two-edged sword, piercing even to the division of soul and spirit . . . . . " Hebrews 4"12a

We cannot trace the whole story here, but as a result of the sin of Adam all human beings are born "dead in sin". (Ephesians 2:1,5). Our souls and bodies were alive, but not our spirits.

The (human) Spirit

What we discover is that only spirit can commune with Spirit. When you are 'born again' your (human) spirit is born within you. You are now able to communicate and fellowship with God.

The Soul

The 'soul' is made up of three elements, the 'mind', the 'emotions' and the 'will'. Without the direction or control of a new spirit within us, our souls are self-centered rather than God-centered. We can see our soul as the 'personality' that those around us relate to and through which we relate to them.[5]

The (physical) Body

Our bodies communicate with the world around us through the five senses – sight, hearing, smell, taste and touch.

We can think of these three elements of our make-up as three concentric circles. The outer circle – we see as our body, in touch with the world. Within that circle, is a circle as our soul – our personality. Again within that circle – if regenerate, is the innermost circle which we see as our spirit – in touch with God.

Jesus, by and with the Holy Spirit indwells the spirit of every born-again believer.

---

[5] There are places in the Scriptures where occasionally the words 'soul' and 'spirit' overlap in their meaning. But we suggest that usually they are found to indicate two different entities.

Various scriptures in the New Testament point to the redemption of our human nature. The Scriptures reveal that 'Redemption' (freeing from sin and its effects) is past, present and future.

1. Christ redeemed us on the cross (past). That was a 'finished' work. .

2. Our souls are in the process of being redeemed (present).

3. Our bodies await their redemption in the Resurrection at the Last Day (future).

Our new spirits are already made perfect. Our souls are in the process of transformation – primarily through the transforming of our minds (Romans 12:2). Our bodies remain affected by sin and whilst by grace through transformed souls, they become our slaves rather than our masters – they remain in that condition until we leave them in death and have them restored in perfection in the resurrection.

The illustration has been given of a wealthy Roman household in the time of the apostle Paul. First there is the Master of the house. `Then there is his Steward. Finally, there is his Slave(s).

They are likened, in order, as the Spirit, Soul and Body.

When the Master (Spirit) is absent, then the Steward (Soul) does what he thinks is best – or acts in his own interest.

When neither the Master nor the Steward is in control, then the Slave takes over.

If the Master is a good head of the household, he will give good instructions to his Steward. The Steward in turn, if he is a good steward acting on the orders of his master, will be in command of the slave, making sure that he does the work assigned to him.

The spirit of man, indwelt, taught and empowered by the Holy Spirit, will converse with and instruct the soul. The soul in turn keeps the body in obedient service.

If the Master is absent, the Steward must make his own decisions. Without the command or instructions of the Master or the Steward, the Slave may become a dangerous rebel.

"What has all this got to do with Living in the New Covenant?", you may be asking. The short answer is , "More than you might think!" As I hope to show in the following pages.

Chapter 4

Law and Grace

In the Introduction, I indicated that the main purpose of this book was to indicate a problem found among many Christians, namely, that they still have 'one foot in the Old Covenant'.

I have further suggested that this may well be because that they have been influenced by that 'dualistic' spirituality – so find themselves living under condemnation rather than the liberty which is theirs in Christ.. They have thought of their souls and bodies to be at war continually, and more frequently than not, it has been a losing battle! At best there is a temporary truce in being.

Now I am not suggesting that there is no element of warfare in the Christian life. There is! But it is a warfare in which we are meant to be "more than conquerors"!

"Yet in all these things we are more than conquerors through Him who loved us." Romans 8:37

How do we come to be "more than conquerors"? It is of course, "through Him who loved us!" But Paul shows us that there is a path by which we come. His whole Letter to the Romans sets out that path.

I can only give a brief outline by way of summary here and if you are not familiar with his Letter, then I urge you to make a careful study of it.

 Paul's intention in his letter is to set out the Gospel of salvation and clearly show how it applies in the life of a believer, whether Jew or Gentile. He starts by showing that we are justified – set right in God's sight - by grace through faith **alone** (without works). He then
36

shows that all are sinners in need of this salvation. After showing Abraham to be an example he leads us to see five freedoms:

1. Freedom from the WRATH of God. Romans 5:1-21

2. Freedom from SIN. Romans 6:1-23

3. Freedom from the LAW. Romans 7:1-25

4. Freedom to Walk in the Spirit – free from CONDEMNATION, the power of SIN and DEATH. Romans 8.

5. Freedom to experience THE TRANSFORMED LIFE in Christ. Romans 12:1 – 15:13

These 'Freedoms' are the spiritual birthright of all true believers. To have some certainty that you are living in the fullness of your birthright, there are a number of questions you can ask yourself.

Chapter 5

Entangled or Free?

In the Introduction we made the point that the apostle Paul wrote in his letter to the Galatians, that they were in danger of being *"entangled with a yoke of bondage"* (Galatians 5:1). They continue to be the "wretched man (or woman)" described by Paul in his letter to the Romans. (Romans 7:13-25 see especially verse 24).

This part of Chapter 7 of Romans (verse 13-25) - known as "The Wretched Man" teaching,- has been the subject of much debate and disagreement among evangelical Christians. Many have taught that it is a description of the **present** condition of every believer. If that is so, then Romans 6 and Romans 8 make little sense! Others, like myself, have come to see that Paul is using the personal "I" as the "historic present tense". This way of speaking is attributed to

Jesus in his telling of parables. If your English Grammar is not up to much, let me explain.

We do not use this normally as a form of speech today, except perhaps in the telling of stories to little children.

"Little Red-Riding-Hood is coming into the woods. It is very dark and she is feeling a bit frightened. But now she is coming to the cottage. She is opening the door and suddenly she sees the wolf is there!"

The past event (historic) is told as though it is taking place now.

Paul did not **continue** to be a wretched man under the law. He was one who through Christ Jesus knew the victory which he spells out. The victory is ours by purchase, by Christ on the Cross. Who delivered Paul? Christ! Who delivers us? Christ!

Let's begin to ask the questions by which we can examine ourselves. Here we present pairs of

40

statements A and B. The questions we ask is, "Which of these statements are the ones we might affirm."? It will become obvious that we need to find our way **out of A** and **into B** in each case.

A: God's people confess their sins to God in order to be forgiven.

B: God's people know that all their sins, past present and future have already been freely forgiven.

A: God removes His presence from His people when they sin.

B: God's people are the temple of the Holy Spirit and their bodies are temples of the Holy Spirit. God will never leave them.

A: God's people are under the Law.

B: God's people are under grace.

A: Go's people believe that sin separates them from God.

B: God's people believe that nothing can ever separate them from the love of God.

A: God's people serve in order to be righteous.

B: God's people are clothed in the righteousness of Christ and so they serve.

A: God's people are progressively sanctified by keeping God's law.

B: God's people are saved by grace and sanctified by grace and progressively transformed by grace into the image of Christ.

A: God's people still have wicked hearts that are deceitful above all things.

B: God's people have been given new hearts and their hearts of stone have been removed.

A: God's people try their best to become godly.

B: God's people are godly. They are accounted perfect in God's sight and are enabled to live godly lives by His grace.

A: God's people have been granted eternal life, but in this world remain "wretched men" awaiting deliverance from sin.

B: God's people have been saved from the penalty and power of sin and by God's grace know victory over the power of sin.

A: God's people fight for victory.

B: God's people fight from the place of victory.

A: God's people keep seeking for more of God.

B: God's people are complete in all the fullness of Christ.

A: God's people keep asking for guidance.

B: God's people have been given the Holy Spirit to indwell them and lead them into all truth.

A: God's people call themselves 'sinners saved by grace'.

B: God's people are never called sinners anywhere in the New Testament, but are frequently addressed as 'saints'.

A: God's people continue to earn acceptance with God and blessings from Him.

B: God's people are already fully accepted by God. He cannot love them more than He does. Nor can He ever love them less.

A: God's people go to church to meet with God and worship Him.

B: God's people are the church and He is ever present to receive our worship.

A: God's people observe Sunday as a Christian Sabbath Day.

B: God's people know Christ as their sabbath rest which they enjoy every day.

A: God's people try to change the world to godly ways to know His blessing upon each nation.

B: God's people know that Christ's kingdom is not of this world and they are called to separate themselves from worldly ways.

A: God's people individually repented of their sins and turned to God in faith and so were born again.

B: God's people were individually born again and having spiritual life, they repented of their sins and believed in Christ.

A: God's people ask God to send them out as disciples to make converts..

B: God's people know that from the moment of conversion they became disciples of Jesus, called to go and make disciples.

A: God's people invite others to repent and believe the Gospel.

B: God's people proclaim the Word of God that commands men and women to repent and believe the Gospel.

A: God's people repeat the "Lord's Prayer" asking God to forgive their sins as they forgive others.

B: God's people know that their forgiveness is unconditional. They thank God for their complete forgiveness through the blood of Christ.

A: God's people "pray the Psalms" as they are found under the Old Covenant.

B: God's people may "pray the Psalms" but always through the change that the New Covenant grants them.

A: God's people believe that every word of Scripture is equally inspired and acceptable for them.

B: God's people believe that every word of Scripture is equally inspired within the progressive revelation of God. So the Old Testament will be seen through the lens of the New Testament.

A: God's people beg and plead with God to make wrong things right.

B: God's people know that He makes all things work together for good for those who love Him and are called according to His good purpose.

A: God's people expect to go to heaven one day.

B: God's people are already seated with Christ in heavenly places and one day will see His glory in the new heaven and the new earth.

A: God's people pray to God to give them their daily bread.

B: God's people thank God for His promised provision of all they need.

A: God's people can become possessed by evil spirits.

47

B: God's people may find themselves oppressed by evil spirits but greater is He who is in them than he who is in the world.

A: God's people confess that without Christ they can do nothing

B: God's people confess that with Christ they can do all things.

A: God's people have priests and ministers who serve them.

B: God's people are all kings and priests unto God.

A: God's people will feel that God is disappointed with them at times.

B: God's people realise that God knows all their weaknesses and sympathises with them, loving them always unconditionally.

We could go adding many more comparisons, but by this time I'm sure you will have got the message!

To live as a Christian believing and acting on all or even some of the "A"s is to live with at least one foot in the Old Covenant.

Chapter 6

Conclusion

I trust it will be obvious, that we are to live with both feet in the New Covenant. Note the following by the writer to the Letter to the Hebrews :

"For this is the covenant that I will make with the house of Israel after those days, says the Lord: I will put My laws in their mind and write them on their hearts; and I will be their God, and they shall be My people. None of them shall teach his neighbour, and none his brother, saying, 'Know the Lord,' for all shall know Me, from the least of them to the greatest of them. For I will be merciful to their unrighteousness, and their sins and their lawless deeds I will remember no more."

In that He says, *"A new covenant,"* **He has made the first obsolete. Now what is becoming obsolete and growing old is ready to vanish away**." Hebrews 8:10-13

The promises of the New Covenant far outweigh those of the Old Covenant which have now become obsolete.

"For the law was given through Moses, but grace and truth came through Jesus Christ." John 1:17

In verse 16 of John Chapter 1 we read that *"Of His (Jesus) fullness we have all received."*

Our need is to realise that and live in the strength of it. We as believers are, or should be, living on the victory side! Salvation by grace through faith is not something merely at the beginning of our Christian walk, it is the on-going reality of our present life in Christ and will take us step by step to glory.

Confess what you are in Christ. You were washed in the blood of Christ when you began. You are

52

constantly washed and cleansed in the blood now. You were clothed in His righteousness then. You are clothed in His righteousness now. You will never be without that robe to cover you.

We wage our warfare from a position of unconquerable strength. We are God's sons, God's warriors. Confess with the apostle Paul that *we are more than conquerors through Him who loved us.* (Romans 8:37)

Be What You Are in Christ

Finally, let me point out that it is vitally important that we make the distinction between **Fellowship** and **Relationship** with God.

Our Fellowship with God can, and may at times, be diminished or even broken., But...

Our Relationship with God can never be changed, diminished or broken. It remains forever the same.

We can liken this to our relationship and fellowship with our natural parents. I am the son of my father. It may be that I enjoy deep fellowship with him. Or I may be estranged from him. But that does not alter the fact that I am his son.

The relationship of the believer with God in Christ will never change,. This is the basis of ever renewable fellowship in His love.

Appendix A

In the introduction, I suggested that if you are unfamiliar with 'evangelical' ways of thinking, especially about being 'born again', you should read this appendix.

What then does it mean to be 'born again'? (Another word for it is 'regeneration'.) The other question that follows is, "How is someone 'born again'?" We need to see what the Bible teaches us about this.

Jesus was asked these two questions by a ruler of the Jews, called Nicodemus. We suggest you read the account in John's Gospel, Chapter 3, verses 1-21.

From this account we learn that it is essential for any individual to be born again, if he or she is to see or to enter the Kingdom of God – the realm in which God lives and rules. To fail to enter that kingdom means that one remains in the kingdom of darkness and of Satan (Colossians 1:13 Ephesians 2: 1-3)

We also learn from the scriptures that until the new birth takes place, one is spiritually dead. (Ephesians 2:1,5 Colossians 2:13) By natural birth we are made up of body and soul. Our soul consists of our mind, emotions (or affections) and wills. Through our bodies we communicate with the world and with our souls we communicate with our bodies. But until we are given new spirits we are unable to communicate with God. (1 Corinthians 2:14). However in the New Covenant in Jesus' blood, we are promised a new heart and a new spirit. (Ezekiel 11:19 Jeremiah 31-37) With our new – born again – spirit we can know and communicate with God.

Adam, in the garden of Eden was told by God that in the day that he ate the fruit of the forbidden tree, he would surely die. (Genesis 2: 17) but we note that his soul and body continued to live. It was his spirit that died. He no longer was in fellowship with God. It is with the fallen nature of Adam that we are born into this world.

Jesus told Nicodemus, "That which is born of the flesh is flesh and that which is born of the Spirit is spirit. " (John 3:7) So spiritual birth is needed.

GOd's Plan of Redemption

God's whole plan to redeem men and women from their lost spiritual state, is through the finished work of Jesus on the cross. Through the suffering, death, burial and resurrection of Jesus – by being spiritually immersed (baptised) into Him – we are given this new nature.

This is what the gospel – the good news – is about. Note what Paul wrote in Ephesians 2:8 and 9

"For by grace you have been saved through faith, and that not of yourselves it is the gift of God, not of works, lest anyone should boast."

Salvation is by **grace** – that is by God's unmerited favour, which means we cannot save ourselves by our good deeds, religious rites or practices.

One example of a person being born again and coming to faith in Christ is the Philippian jailer in Acts Chapter 16. He asked, " What must I do to be saved ?." Paul's answer was that he simply needed to " Believe on the Lord Jesus Christ".

When the Holy Spirit comes to someone through the preaching or sharing of the gospel , they are given a new heart. From their new heart they will repent of their sins and believe in Jesus that he died for them personally. They received Him as their Lord and Saviour. They have been born again !

As a new disciple he or she will need to be baptised (immersed) in water to show that they have died to an old life and risen to a new one. They will need to feed on the Word of God in the

Bible in order to grow. This will be through joining with other Christians.

The Author

Fred Serjeant has been married to Mary for sixty years, and they have three sons, six grandchildren and one great-grandson. Fred has been in pastoral and evangelistic ministry for 65 years. He is the author four other books published through Amazon:

"Understanding the New Covenant" A Simple Introduction the New Covenant Theology

"Make Disciples!" Making Disciples who Make Disciples. A Discipleship Manual

"12 Steps Out" A Manual for Freedom from Addiction

'**The Twelve Pillars of the Christian Faith**"
Twelve Key Doctrines that uphold the Gospel of
Grace

These are all available from Amazon.co.uk (If
you live in the U.K.) or from Amazon.com
worldwide. Some of them are also available as
Kindle versions.

If you have questions you would like to ask about
the contents of this book, or any of the others,
please   go   to   the   website   at
www.simplechurch.org.uk for contact details.

28215930R00036

Printed in Poland
by Amazon Fulfillment
Poland Sp. z o.o., Wrocław